AMAZING
MATH

First edition for the United States and Canada published in 2018 by Barron's Educational Series, Inc.

Text, design, and illustrations copyright © Carlton Books Limited 2018, an imprint of the Carlton Publishing Group, 20 Mortimer Street, London, W1T 3JW

All inquiries should be addressed to:
Barron's Educational Series, Inc.
250 Wireless Boulevard
Hauppauge, NY 11788
www.barronseduc.com

ISBN: 978-1-4380-1250-6

Date of Manufacture: July 2018
Manufactured by: RRD Asia, Dongguan, China

Printed in China
9 8 7 6 5 4 3 2 1

Executive editor: Bryony Davies
Design: Kate Wiliwinska
Designed and illustrated by: Dynamo Limited
Picture research: Steve Behan and Paul Langan
Production: Nicola Davey

AUTHOR:

HANNAH WILSON has edited and written children's nonfiction for 20 years. With a particular interest in STEM, she has made more than 100 titles—books about astronauts and space, the human body, technology, and the natural world, in addition to revision guides and science-based reading plans. She has written many titles about animals, including Carlton's *iExplore Bugs*, which won a best book award at the Bologna Book Fair 2018 (Ragazzi Digital Award).

STEM EDITORIAL CONSULTANT:
MARGARET (MEG) KÄUFER is a founding member and current president of the STEM Alliance of Larchmont-Mamaroneck, NY. The STEM Alliance is a nonprofit organization with the mission of creating a network of STEM learning opportunities to connect today's youth to the jobs of the future. They work closely with local schools to run hands-on, applied STEM enrichment experiences. Highlights of their work under her leadership include launching an annual public STEM festival, establishing competitive robotics teams, and creating a hands-on STEM summer enrichment program for at-risk children. Meg has her Masters in Curriculum & Instruction from Teachers College, Columbia University. Throughout her career, Meg has championed STEM learning for its capacity to engage and inspire all varieties of learners.

PICTURE ACKNOWLEDGMENTS
The publishers would like to thank the following sources for their kind permission to reproduce the pictures in the book.

Pages 6–7: Alexandr III/Shutterstock; 10–11 (background): Aklionka/Shutterstock; 12 (top right): Public Domain; 13 (right): MicroOne/Shutterstock; 14–15 (background): Inspiring/Shutterstock; 14 (bottom left): Kirill Kirsanov/Shutterstock; 16 (hamster): Kuttelvaserova Stuchelova/Shutterstock, (cat): Peter Wollinga/Shutterstock, (dog): Cynoclub/Shutterstock; 18–19 (background): Kelvin Degree/Shutterstock; 19 (bottom left): Studio_G/Shutterstock; 23 (center): VectorPixelStar/Shutterstock, (bottom): Mary Terriberry/Shutterstock; 24 (bottom right): Attaphong/Shutterstock; 29 (left): 89studio/Shutterstock, (right): Lekkystockphoto/Shutterstock; 30 (smart phone): Stanisic Vladimir/Shutterstock; 32–33 (clock face): Attaphong/Shutterstock; 34 (top right): Harlowbutler/Shutterstock; 40–41 (butterflies): Butterfly Hunter/Shutterstock; 41 (notebook): 89studio/Shutterstock; 45 (top right): NASA/Donaldson Collection/Getty Images; 49 (top right): Fine Art Images/Heritage Images/Getty Images; 52 (top right): Attaphong/Shutterstock; 53 (bottom right): Public Domain; 54 (top left): Kudla/Shutterstock, (top right): Ketpachara Yoosuk/Shutterstock, (center): Mega Pixel/Shutterstock, (bottom): Stockphoto-graf/Shutterstock; 60 (bottom right): Daniel Prudek/Shutterstock

Every effort has been made to acknowledge correctly and contact the source and/or copyright holder of each picture, and Carlton Books apologizes for any unintentional errors or omissions, which will be corrected in future editions of this book.

STEM ADVENTURES

AMAZING
MATH

Hannah Wilson

BARRON'S

CONTENTS

SUPER STEM

Welcome to the world of STEM. STEM stands for science, technology, engineering, and math. These four fabulous subjects open up a world of exciting discovery.

You probably already possess many of the qualities and interests shared by great scientists, technologists, engineers, and mathematicians. Read each statement and put a check in the box if it applies to you.

SCIENCE

YOU...

- are curious about the world around you. ☐

- love to ask questions. ☐

- experiment and try new things, even if it means making a mistake. ☐

You're already on your way to becoming a scientist! You're excited to discover more about the way scientists think and work.

TECHNOLOGY

YOU...

- are always playing with gadgets. ☐

- like to understand exactly how machines work. ☐

- try to find ways of making everyday tasks easier, such as investigating whether a different route to school makes the trip shorter. ☐

Technology is right up your alley! You're fascinated by the latest products and want to find out more about inventions that help improve our world.

ENGINEERING

YOU...

- like using your brain to solve problems. ☐

- love playing with construction sets and building blocks. ☐

- enjoy building amazing dens or dams in streams. ☐

You're perfectly suited to a career as an engineer! You could invent or make amazing tools, machines, and buildings.

MATH

YOU...

- like to understand the reasons why something is true. ☐

- often spot patterns in pictures and clothing or sequences in numbers like football statistics. ☐

- love 3-D puzzles, card games, and logic games like chess. ☐

You're a born mathematician! You're excited by shapes and measurements and curious to see what numbers can do when you use them in different ways.

WHAT IS MATH?

Math is around us, all the time. We use it to help keep track of the money we spend, to score sports matches, to calculate quantities for cooking, to build skyscrapers, and to organize maps.

Math also reveals the secrets of the natural world—for example, it explains the spiral patterns of seashells and the symmetry of honeycombs.

Numbers are the symbols we use to describe math. When linked with other symbols, such as + or − and =, they create a unique international language. In this book, we're going to learn how to read and write the language of math so we can explore and understand the world around us. So, let's get started—we have shapes to draw, numbers to juggle, codes to decipher, treasure maps to study, computers to program, and pizzas to slice!

COOL COLUMNS

A number describes an amount of something. It can be written as a word, like "eight," or with digits, like "8" or "2." Digits are a faster way to write a large number. For example, it's much quicker to write "2,917" than it is to write "two thousand nine hundred and seventeen!"

Each digit in a number shows how many you have of a particular value—thousands, hundreds, tens, and ones (or units). This is the digit's "place value." The columns below show the value of each digit in the number 2,917.

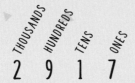

THOUSANDS HUNDREDS TENS ONES

2 9 1 7

There are 2 thousands, 9 hundreds, 1 ten, and 7 ones.

We can expand 2,917 so it becomes 2,000 + 900 + 10 + 7.

ACTIVITY

Write these numbers in expanded form.

3,725

4,159

7,022

ACTIVITY

Can you find your way out of this number maze? Travel from number to number, but make sure the numbers get bigger each time, not smaller!

4   7
22   29
11   16

4   2
1   2
46   37
2
4   2   85   78
97   92   44   56
7   4
99   37   46
3   7   32   34   35
11   16   67   56
16   22
22   29
27   29

Look at the numbers you connected to make your way through the maze. How much is added to each one to get the next number in the sequence? What pattern can you see?

CHECK THE ANSWERS AT THE BACK OF THE BOOK!

SUPER SUMS

When adding or subtracting numbers, we use symbols to record our math.

Means "add on" or "plus"

Means "is equal to"

$3 + 2 = 5$
$3 - 2 = 1$

Means "take away," "minus," or "subtract"

You also need to know some rules about how to write things down in a calculation...

ORDER RULE: ADDING

When adding, the order of the numbers doesn't matter. You can write the numbers on either side of the + symbol. For example:

$3 + 2 = 5$
$2 + 3 = 5$

ORDER RULE: SUBTRACTING

The order of the numbers does matter for subtraction. For example, $3 - 2 = 1$, but if you swap the order so the calculation is $2 - 3$, the answer is not 1!

ACTIVITY

Look at these road signs and figure out the distances between the different destinations. All the distances shown are in straight lines.

SCHOOL	2
TRAIN STATION	7
HOSPITAL	10

PARK	13
BUS STATION	18
SUPERMARKET	20

How many miles are there between the school and the train station?

How many miles are there between the park and the bus station?

What's the distance between the train station and the hospital?

What's the distance between the bus station and the supermarket?

How far is it from the school to the hospital?

How far is it from the park to the supermarket?

CHECK THE ANSWERS AT THE BACK OF THE BOOK!

POPULATION COUNT

The population of the town of Addington is being counted in a survey! Population surveys help make sure that towns like Addington have the right number of services, such as schools and hospitals. Help out with the survey by adding up the number of people living in each building.

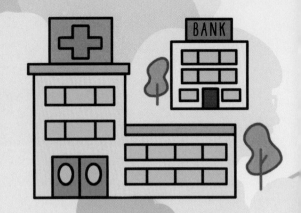

ADDITION WITH REGROUPING

For tricky addition with numbers that have several digits, organize the numbers in columns according to their place value, like the example below.

```
HUNDREDS  TENS  ONES
    1       1
            6     7
     +      8     5
    ───────────────
    1       5     2
```

HERE'S HOW TO DO IT:

· Add up the ones first: 7 + 5 = 12.

· Record the digit 2 in the ones place.

· You have created 1 new "ten," so carry that over into the tens place.

· Now add up the tens, including the 1 that you carried over: 6 + 8 + 1 = 15.

· 15 tens is 1 group of hundreds and 5 tens. Record the 5 in the tens place and carry over the 1 into the hundreds place.

· Now add the hundreds.

· The answer is 152.

ACTIVITY

Add up the number of people living on all the floors in each building, and write the total in the space in the bottom of each house.

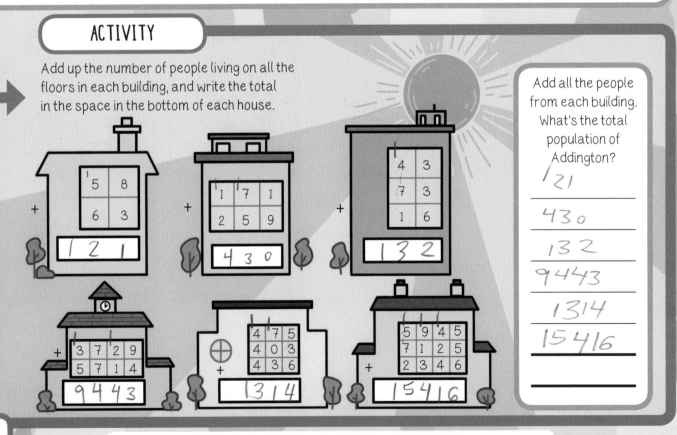

Add all the people from each building. What's the total population of Addington?

121
430
132
9443
1314
15416

CHECK THE ANSWERS AT THE BACK OF THE BOOK!

SUBTRACTION WITH REGROUPING

Welcome to Subtractington! People are moving out of this town. Use subtraction to figure out how many residents are left in each building.

```
    TENS ONES
      8⁄9 ¹2
    -  6  4
    ─────────
       2  8
```

HERE'S HOW TO DO IT:

· Start with the ones place. Because you can't take 4 ones away from 2, you need to borrow from the tens column.

· Borrow 1 ten from the tens column by crossing out the 9 and reducing it to 8 tens.

· Write the borrowed ten as a 1 next to the 2 in the ones place (as shown) to get 12 ones.

· You can now subtract: 12 − 4 = 8. Put 8 in the ones place.

· Now work on the tens column: 8 − 6 = 2.

· The answer is 28.

ACTIVITY

Subtract the number of people who are leaving from the number of people who live in each building. Write the answer in the space in the bottom of each house.

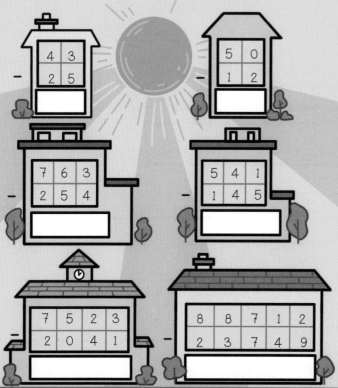

```
  4 3
- 2 5
```

```
  5 0
- 1 2
```

```
  7 6 3
- 2 5 4
```

```
  5 4 1
- 1 4 5
```

```
  7 5 2 3
- 2 0 4 1
```

```
  8 8 7 1 2
- 2 3 7 4 9
```

Add the total remaining residents to figure out the population of Subtractington.

_____

_____

_____

_____

_____

_____

How many more people live in Subtractington than Addington?

_____

_____

_____

ABOVE AND BELOW ZERO

Numbers above zero are "positive." But if you count down from ten to zero, you don't need to stop there. Numbers below zero are "negative" numbers. We show that a number is negative by putting a minus symbol – in front of it.

We can use negative numbers when we talk about temperature, which drops below zero when it's very cold. Brrr! In the Antarctic, for example, temperatures struggle to get above −4 degrees Fahrenheit in the summer. Scientists and other support staff live there to carry out research.

BRAHMAGUPTA

In about 628 C.E., the Indian mathematician Brahmagupta wrote a book in which he treated zero as a proper number that could be used in calculations. Before that, zero had just been used as a symbol when there was no quantity to record, like the zero in 306.

ACTIVITY

Complete this picture of an Antarctic research station by connecting the dots—with a twist! The dots have positive and negative numbers. Start at 15 and count down to −15.

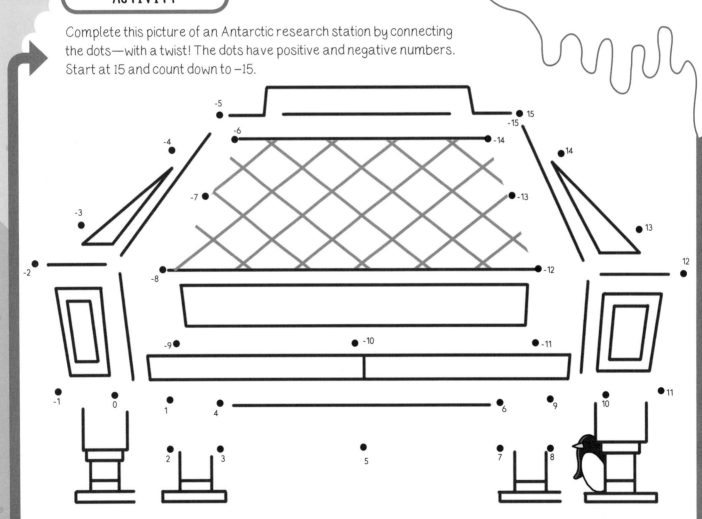

This thermometer shows the temperature in degrees Fahrenheit (°F) and Celsius (°C). During the day, the temperature goes up and down. Using the information below, write down calculations to find out what temperature the thermometer would show at different times. Use your finger to count up and down the thermometer number line to check your answers.

Before dawn, it's 32°F (0°C). The sun rises and the temperature increases by 8 degrees.

At midday, an ice storm hits, and the temperature drops by 11 degrees.

The sun comes out again in the afternoon, and the temperature rises by 5 degrees.

Finally, night falls, and the temperature drops by 7 degrees.

DID YOU KNOW?

The lowest ground temperature ever recorded with a thermometer on Earth is −128.6°F (−89°C)! That was in Antarctica in 1983.

°F °C
90
70
50
30
10

30
20
10
0
−10
−20

MULTIPLY AND SUPPLY

Meet the "multiplication" or "times" symbol: ×. Multiplication is very handy if you want to add up the same number many—or multiple—times. If 5 boxes each contain 3 pencils, how many pencils are there in total? To work this out, we need to add $3 + 3 + 3 + 3 + 3 = 15$. Or you could use the × symbol to write $5 × 3 = 15$.

ORDER RULE: MULTIPLYING

You can multiply numbers in any order. For example:

$5 × 3 = 15$
$3 × 5 = 15$

DID YOU KNOW?

On a calculator, computer, or smartphone, the multiplication symbol is often *.

ACTIVITY

Your company makes sports equipment. Three orders for equipment have come in. How much does each customer owe?

To calculate the bill, multiply the number ordered by the price.

ORDER	TOTAL PRICE
SUMMER CAMP 2 packs of frisbees	2 x $8 =
SPORTING GOODS STORE 2 crates of basketballs	
SCHOOL 2 tubes of tennis balls	

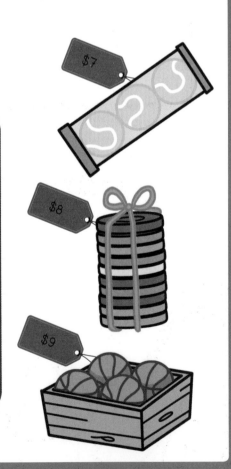

$7

$8

$9

CHECK THE ANSWERS AT THE BACK OF THE BOOK!

MULTIPLICATION

For tricky multiplication problems with more than one digit, write your numbers in columns.

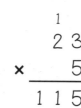

```
    1
    2 3
×     5
─────────
  1 1 5
```

- First, multiply the number in the ones place: 3 × 5 = 15.
- You have created a new "ten," so carry the 1 over into the tens place.
- Now multiply the tens value: 2 × 5 = 10.
- Add the regrouped 1, which makes 11.
- The answer is 115.

ACTIVITY

The phone rings. The summer camp wants to double its order, the sporting goods store wants to triple its order, and the school wants to quadruple its order! Use multiplication to multiply each one's first bill total by the increased amount.

SUMMER CAMP

Total of new bill: $ _____

SPORTING GOODS STORE

Total of new bill: $ _____

SCHOOL

Total of new bill: $ _____

MEET THE MULTIPLES

Multiples are a way of counting by a number in a series. When you count by 5s, you're multiplying by 5s. Counting 5, 10, 15, 20 is the same as $(5 \times 1) = 5$, $(5 \times 2) = 10$, $(5 \times 3) = 15$, and so on. Multiples are useful everywhere, even when shopping.

ACTIVITY

Vera the veterinarian needs food for her animal shelter. Help her count in multiples along each aisle to find the quantities on her shopping list. Circle the boxes as you count, and note the numbers on her shopping list.

Hamster food
1 box $10
(2 bags each)

Cat food
1 box $6
(6 cans each)

Dog bones
1 box $4
(7 bones each)

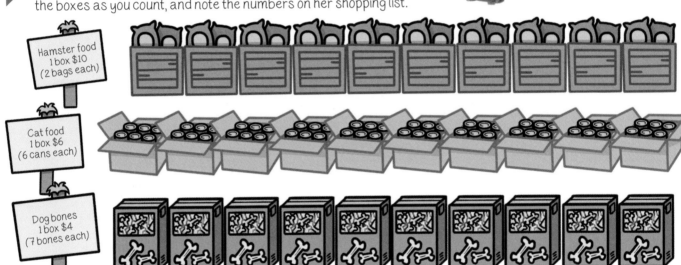

SHOPPING LIST

14 bags of hamster food = ⬚ boxes of hamster food

30 cans of cat food = ⬚ boxes of cat food

42 dog bones = ⬚ boxes of dog bones

Put the number of boxes needed in the first column. Write the price per item in the price column. Multiply the amount by the price to get the cost for each type of food.

NUMBER OF BOXES	PRICE	TOTAL
	GRAND TOTAL:	

Use multiples of 3 and 8 to find out which animals are hiding in the grassland! Choose a colored pencil and then connect the dots, starting at 3 and counting up in multiples of 3.

Then use a different color and start at 8. Connect the dots that are multiples of 8.

Finish by coloring the scene.

17

SHARE AND DIVIDE

When you want to share, use division to help you. For this, we use the ÷ symbol. Division breaks a number into equal amounts. For example, 8 ÷ 2 means to divide 8 into two equal amounts.

ORDER RULE: DIVIDING

The order of the numbers matters when you use division.

For example, 8 ÷ 2 = 4, but if you swap the order and write 2 ÷ 8, the answer is not 4!

ACTIVITY

Five friends are getting ready for an outdoor adventure. Three are going fishing and two will make a tent.

1 FOOD FOR ALL FIVE FRIENDS

5 WATER BOTTLES

10 ENERGY BARS

55 GRAPES

15 BANANAS

2 GEAR FOR THREE FISHERS

12 WORMS

6 HOOKS

3 GEAR FOR TWO TENT MAKERS

26 STICKS

6 COILS OF ROPE

Pack a backpack for one of the fishers and one of the tent makers. Use division to figure out how much they need of each item. Remember, the snacks are shared by all five friends. The fishing gear is shared by three friends. The tent gear is shared by two friends.

WRITE A LIST OF ITEMS FOR EACH BACKPACK HERE

FISHER'S BACKPACK		TENT MAKER'S BACKPACK	
1	water bottles	1	water bottles
2	energy bars	2	energy bars
11	grapes	11	grapes
3	bananas	3	bananas
4	worms	13	sticks
2	hooks	3	coils of rope

CHECK THE ANSWERS AT THE BACK OF THE BOOK!

DIVISION

To divide a large number, divide each digit in each place value separately. Look at this example of $324 \div 2$ using place values.

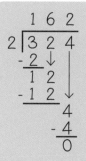

```
    1 6 2
  2│3 2 4
   -2↓
    1 2
   -1 2↓
        4
       -4
        0
```

Start in the hundreds place. The 2 goes into 3 with 1 left over. We call the 1 the "remainder." It creates an extra "ten," so now we are dividing 2 into 12 in the tens place. 12 divided by 2 is 6 with no remainder.

There are 4 ones in the ones place. 4 divided by 2 is 2.

$$200 \div 10 = 20$$
$$2,000 \div 10 = 200$$
$$20,000 \div 10 = 2,000$$

Do you see a pattern? When you divide by 10, you drop a zero.

When you divide by 100, you drop two zeros:

$$200 \div 100 = 2$$

ACTIVITY

It's time to toast marshmallows on the campfire! The five children have three bags of marshmallows, each containing 26 marshmallows. Use division to share the marshmallows between all five friends.

How many marshmallows are there in total?

```
   2 6
 X   3
 ─────
   7 8
```

How many does each child get if they divide them up equally?

```
      1 5
  5│7 8
    5
    2 8
    2 5
      3
```

```
      7
 10│7 8
    7 0
    ─────
      8 0
```

Are there any left over (remainders)? If so, how many?

3

Five more kids arrive. Now there are 10 kids to share all the marshmallows. Divide the total by 10. How many will each child get?

7

FACTOR FACTORY

The factors of a number are all the numbers that you can multiply together to make that number. So, the factors of 4 are 1 and 4 (1 × 4 = 4) and 2 (2 × 2 = 4). The factors of 6 are 1, 6, 2, and 3. Both 1 and 2 are factors of 4 and 6, so we call them "common factors" of 4 and 6.

FACTORS OF 4

1   2   4

MATH TIP
The factors of a number are always 1 and the number itself. But sometimes there are more!

ACTIVITY

Find the factors of 9, 14, and 21 and write them in the key below. Then use the key to color in the factor factory to see what it's making!

KEY

- ■ Factors of 9   ☐ ☐ ☐
- ■ Factors of 14   ☐ ☐ ☐ ☐
- ■ Factors of 21   ☐ ☐ ☐ ☐

CAN YOU FIND THE GCF?

Look at the factors of 14 and 21. What is the greatest factor that they have in common? That's the "greatest common factor" or GCF.

CHECK THE ANSWERS AT THE BACK OF THE BOOK!

Four teachers are at the bookstore buying books for their classrooms. The books come in packs of 3, 4, 5, and 7.

Mr. 12 needs to buy exactly 12 books. The packs of 3 and 4 books are perfect because those numbers are factors of 12. Mr. 12 could buy four packs of 3 books or three packs of 4 books. Which option would be cheapest?

Help the other teachers find their factors and compare two different pack options. Circle the cheapest option for each teacher.

MR. 12 COULD BUY:

4 × 3-pack of books

4 × $10 = $......

OR

3 × 4-pack of books

3 × $12 = $......

MRS. 15 COULD BUY:

...... × ......-pack of books

...... × $...... = $......

OR

...... × ......-pack of books

...... × $...... = $......

MR. 20 COULD BUY:

...... × ......-pack of books

...... × $...... = $......

OR

...... × ......-pack of books

...... × $...... = $......

MRS. 21 COULD BUY:

...... × ......-pack of books

...... × $...... = $......

OR

...... × ......-pack of books

...... × $...... = $......

CHECK THE ANSWERS AT THE BACK OF THE BOOK!

NUMBERS IN THEIR PRIME

A prime number is a number that can be divided only by itself and 1.
For example, 17 can only be divided by 17 and 1, so 17 is a prime number.
A composite number is a number that can be divided by several numbers.
For example, 20 can be divided by 2, 4, 5, and 10 as well as
20 and 1, so 20 is a composite number.

ACTIVITY

The fish in this pond are either composite or prime numbers. Help Costas and Priya catch the composite numbers by coloring them in. Use the Math Tip box to help you!

MATH TIP

The number 5 is prime, but all numbers ending in 5 are composite. All even numbers are composite except 2. All numbers that can be divided by 3 are composite except 3 itself.

This fussy caterpillar eats only prime numbers up to 50! They are 2, 3, 5, 7, 11, 13, 17, 19, 23, 29, 31, 37, 41, 43, and 47.

Draw a line linking up the prime numbers and help it munch its way through the leaf maze.

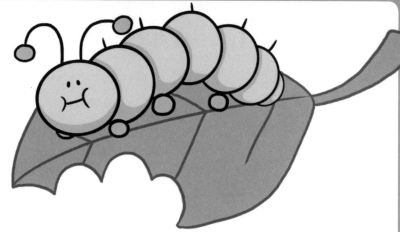

↓ START

2	35	10	14	18	27	9	8	28	50
3	5	7	11	4	39	38	6	20	30
24	34	22	13	23	29	31	40	33	46
32	48	21	17	19	23	37	41	43	45
25	26	44	42	36	49	1	16	47	15

FINISH ↑

DID YOU KNOW?

The number 1 is neither a prime number nor a composite number!

Some cicadas leave their burrows to lay eggs every 7, 13, or 17 years. They may choose these prime-number intervals to avoid predators, whose life-cycles are not based on primes.

CHECK THE ANSWERS AT THE BACK OF THE BOOK!

CRACK THE CODE

A code is a sequence of numbers. We use codes every day in lots of different ways—in the passcodes on our phones, the locks on our bikes, the barcodes on products, and so on. But not all codes are random sequences of numbers. Many are based on math and number patterns.

ACTIVITY

A cybercriminal has hacked into the city bank's computers and transferred all the money to his own account. It's your job to crack the codes. Solve each challenge and use the encryption key on the next page to find out who the criminal is.

1

Write the next number in these sequences.

23, 27, 31, 35, 39, 43

1, 2, 4, 8, 16, 32

20, 15, 11, 8, 6, 5
-5 -4 -3 -2

12, 24, 36, 48, 60, 72

2

Read the riddle below. Which of the three padlocks is it describing?

What do the three numbers on the correct padlock add up to?

7

My second number is double the first. My third is half of the first.

3

HINT
The line always cuts through numbers that are opposite each other.

The line on this clock cuts through numbers 12 and 6, which equal 18 when added together. Rotate the line clockwise until you find two numbers on the clock with a sum that is divisible by 7.

What is the sum of the two numbers that is divisible by 7?

7

Which two numbers make this total?   1   7

Use this answer in the encryption key.

CHECK THE ANSWERS AT THE BACK OF THE BOOK!

4

The Fibonacci sequence is a famous code. It starts like this:

1, 1, 2, 3, 5, 8, 13...

Can you figure out the pattern?

Think about how each number is related to the two numbers before it.

What's the next number in the sequence?

twenty one   21

5

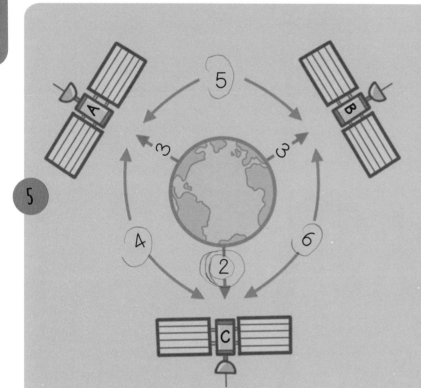

This picture shows how many seconds it takes for messages from Earth to reach different satellites.

What is the quickest route for a message to leave your computer on Earth, travel to all three satellites, and then arrive back on Earth? How long will it take?

Shortest route:

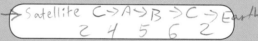
→ Satellite C → A → B → C → Earth
2   4   5   6   2

Time taken:

19 seconds

NOW DISCOVER THE CRIMINAL'S NAME!

A	B	C	D	E	F	G	H	I	J	K	L	M
12	3	21	10	8	37	15	22	32	41	17	5	29

N	O	P	Q	R	S	T	U	V	W	X	Y	Z
74	14	4	24	7	16	1	49	63	43	2	72	61

Use the encryption key above to turn the answers from each challenge into letters, and you'll discover the thief's name.

CHALLENGE 3   CHALLENGE 5

CHALLENGE 1   CHALLENGE 2   CHALLENGE 4

| W | I | L | Y | | R | O | C | O |

FOOD FRACTIONS

A fraction describes how a whole number is divided into equal parts. The pie on the right is divided into three parts. If you eat 2 parts, you've eaten $\frac{2}{3}$ (two-thirds) of the pie.

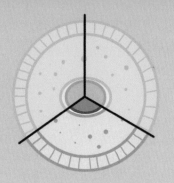

$$2 \quad \longleftarrow \quad \text{Numerator—the number of parts we're talking about}$$

$$\overline{} \quad \longleftarrow \quad \text{Line means "divided by"}$$

$$3 \quad \longleftarrow \quad \text{Denominator—the number of parts in the whole}$$

ACTIVITY

Three friends are sharing a pizza. There are 12 slices, but each person wants a different number of slices. How much does each person get? Color in the slices, using a different color for each person.

If a pizza is divided into 12 slices and we eat all 12 slices, we have eaten $\frac{12}{12}$ of the pizza—that's the whole pizza. So, if the numerator and denominator are the same number, that fraction equals 1.

$$\frac{4}{4} = 1,$$
$$\frac{11}{11} = 1,$$
$$\frac{433}{433} = 1,$$

and so on.

CHUN
"Just $\frac{3}{12}$ for me."

RUBY
"I would like $\frac{6}{12}$ of the pizza."

SANJAY
"I'll have $\frac{2}{12}$ please."

How many slices are left? Write your answer as a fraction.

EQUIVALENT FRACTIONS

Ruby ate 6 out of 12 slices. That was $\frac{1}{2}$ of the pizza. It's the same amount of pizza but broken into fewer pieces because the denominator is smaller.

To simplify a fraction, divide the numerator and denominator by the same number.
So, $\frac{6}{12} = \frac{1}{2}$. They are "equivalent fractions."

$$\frac{6}{12} \overset{\div 6}{\underset{\div 6}{=}} \frac{1}{2}$$

This also works in reverse. You can multiply the numerator and the denominator of a fraction by the same number and get an equivalent fraction.

$$\frac{1}{2} \overset{\times 6}{\underset{\times 6}{=}} \frac{6}{12}$$

ACTIVITY

Each squirrel is looking for a route up the tree that matches his fraction.
Draw a route up the tree for each squirrel, following the equivalent fractions.

Which nut will the $\frac{1}{2}$ squirrel get?

Which nut will the $\frac{1}{3}$ squirrel get?

Which nut will the $\frac{1}{4}$ squirrel get?

DECIMALS THAT DIVIDE

Like fractions, decimals describe how a whole number is divided into parts. A decimal number contains a decimal point that separates the whole number and its fractional parts. Each part is one tenth ($\frac{1}{10}$) of the previous unit. The number to the right of the decimal point is $\frac{1}{10}$ and is written as 0.1. If you divide that tenth into another 10 parts, each of the smaller parts is one hundredth ($\frac{1}{100}$). This is written as 0.01.

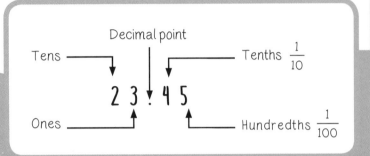

Tens

Decimal point

Tenths $\frac{1}{10}$

2 3 . 4 5

Ones

Hundredths $\frac{1}{100}$

EQUIVALENTS

$0.5 = \frac{5}{10} = \frac{1}{2}$

$0.25 = \frac{25}{100} = \frac{1}{4}$

$0.75 = \frac{75}{100} = \frac{3}{4}$

ACTIVITY

Draw rope bridges between the posts that have equivalent numbers, so Jeff can cross the gorge. One has been done for you already.

$2\frac{1}{2}$

2.5

$9\frac{1}{4}$

$3\frac{1}{4}$

$\frac{3}{4}$

9.25

3.25

9.5

1.75

0.75

2.75

$1\frac{3}{4}$

CHECK THE ANSWERS AT THE BACK OF THE BOOK!

To add decimals, line up the decimal points. Then add each unit. Use regrouping if needed.

Try out addition with decimals. Add up the cost of your groceries. Write down the cost for each item. Make sure the decimal points line up. Then figure out the total cost of your items.

$0.50 $2.30
$1.50
$0.15 $1.75 $0.30 $0.40 $0.75

	Tens	Ones	.	Tenths	Hundredths
BREAD			.		
APPLE			.		
MILK			.		
CHEESE			.		
CEREAL			.		
GARLIC			.		
BROCCOLI			.		
PASTA			.		
TOTAL			.		

You pay for the groceries with a $10 bill. How much change would you get?

There are 100 pennies in $1, so the decimal system is perfect for writing amounts of money.

If you have $2 and 53 pennies, it's written as $2.53, because in addition to 2 whole dollars, you have 53 hundredths of 1 dollar.

If you have only 2 pennies, that's $0.02 or 2 hundredths of a dollar. You don't have any whole dollars.

PERCENTAGES

Percentages, like fractions and decimals, describe part of a whole number.
Percent (%) means "out of 100." So, 50% means 50 out of 100 or $\frac{50}{100}$.

ACTIVITY

When you receive data on your computer or phone, it doesn't arrive as a whole package. It is broken into pieces. Your device tells you how much of the whole package you have received. The messages below come in 10 parts. Color in the loading screens to match the percentages.

HINT: You don't have to color in whole squares.

Halfway there!

LOADING...50%

Thanks for waiting!

LOADING...25%

Almost fully loaded!

LOADING...90%

Not long now!

LOADING...75%

CHECK THE ANSWERS AT THE BACK OF THE BOOK!

Connect each flag with its correct boat.

50% GIRLS
25% BOYS
25% DOGS

20% DOGS
50% GIRLS
30% BOYS

50% DOGS
25% GIRLS
25% BOYS

ACTIVITY

Draw lines to connect each food item with the right percentage, decimal, and fraction to show how much food or drink there is.

25%
$\frac{25}{100} = \frac{1}{4}$
0.25

75%
$\frac{75}{100} = \frac{3}{4}$
0.75

50%
$\frac{5}{10} = \frac{1}{2}$
0.5

CHECK THE ANSWERS AT THE BACK OF THE BOOK!

WHAT'S THE TIME?

What time do you wake up? What time does school start? When do you need to be at the dentist? How many hours until the party starts? Getting anywhere on time means learning how to read a clock!

REMEMBER. THERE ARE:

60 seconds in a minute

60 minutes in an hour

24 hours in a day

DID YOU KNOW

The long hand on an analog clock points to the minute and the short hand points to the hour.

Minutes are grouped together in sets of five.

Often, we say "quarter past seven" when we mean 15 minutes past seven. This is because 15 minutes is $\frac{1}{4}$ of 60 minutes, or a quarter of an hour. "Quarter to seven" means 15 minutes before seven.

"Half past seven" means 30 minutes past seven—$\frac{1}{2}$ of 60 minutes.

ACTIVITY

Draw the hands on the clocks to keep track of time during this busy day.

1 Wakey, wakey! It's 7 o'clock in the morning.

2 Eat breakfast at half past seven.

3 Catch the bus at quarter past eight.

4 School starts at quarter to nine.

7 Swimming lesson at quarter to twelve.

8 Are you hungry? Lunch is at 1:00.

14 It's 8:35. Good night!

9 Your soccer game is at 2:40 p.m.

13 Read a book in bed at five past eight.

6 Head to the playground for recess at 10:15 a.m.

10 Start your homework at twenty minutes to four.

5 It's half past nine—time for a math lesson!

$2+12\div3\times5=$

12 It's half past seven. Time to take a bath.

11 Eat dinner at 6:15 p.m.

CHECK THE ANSWERS AT THE BACK OF THE BOOK!

ROMAN NUMERALS

The ancient Romans used letter symbols to represent numbers. We still sometimes use these Roman numerals, especially on clock faces.

ROMAN RULES

For smaller numbers, you just need to recognize three letter symbols:

$$1 = I \qquad 5 = V \qquad 10 = X$$

When a smaller number appears after a larger one, add the two together: VI = 5 + 1, so VI = 6. XI is 11.

When a smaller number appears before a larger one, subtract the smaller number from the larger one: IV = 5 − 1, so IV is 4. IX is 9.

You can write all the numbers between 1 and 49 in Roman numerals using just these three symbols.

20 = XX	60 = LX	100 = C
30 = XXX	70 = LXX	500 = D
40 = XL	80 = LXXX	1000 = M
50 = L	90 = XC	

ACTIVITY

Help the soldier find his way back to camp by following Roman numerals in increasing order from I to XX. Beware of dead ends!

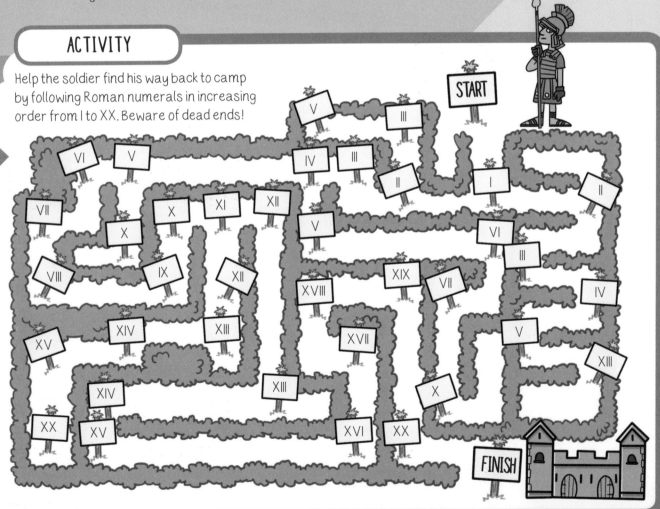

CHECK THE ANSWERS AT THE BACK OF THE BOOK!

Roman numerals were hard to use in calculations because there were no columns for thousands, hundreds, tens, and ones—and there were no zeros! For 2,000, the Romans simply wrote M twice: MM. This meant that simple numbers could be really long!

The numbers below are years shown in Roman numerals. Can you figure out the year that they represent? Use the box on page 34 to help you.

1. MMX

2. MMXXIX

3. MMLXIV

Today, we use the Hindu-Arabic number system to write 2,000—a number that's easy to write and easy to use in calculations like adding and subtracting.

Below are historical events. Write each year in Roman numerals. Then find the year in the grid and circle it. The first one is done for you.

1. The city of Rome was founded in 753 B.C.E.

DCCLIII

2. The Great Fire of Rome took place in 64 C.E.

3. Rome's Colosseum was completed in about 80 C.E.

4. Rome split into Eastern and Western Empires in 395 C.E.

C	D	T	I	R	E	V	S	G	J	J	K	K
M	N	X	H	I	V	X	I	V	F	D	X	Z
O	P	C	L	K	M	J	U	H	N	E	B	Y
T	G	F	V	L	D	E	R	V	X	H	F	V
D	S	X	C	U	Y	H	J	N	B	G	T	F
V	F	R	D	C	C	L	I	I	I	B	O	P
L	M	N	W	B	V	C	X	Z	A	S	D	F
G	X	H	Q	I	V	X	R	V	T	L	D	E
V	I	X	Q	O	P	V	L	X	K	X	I	M
N	X	I	L	V	F	D	C	W	X	S	Z	M
Q	E	W	U	U	I	V	J	K	U	Y	G	L
R	F	C	E	X	I	Q	A	I	X	V	V	X
N	M	C	H	G	F	U	Y	I	O	I	L	I
J	M	C	H	G	M	L	X	X	X	C	V	V
W	Q	X	S	X	Z	X	C	V	C	B	N	M
J	K	C	I	V	U	C	P	K	J	L	H	N
B	G	V	V	C	D	R	E	S	D	X	C	X

MEASURING METRIC

The metric system is a system of measurement that uses meters to measure length, grams to measure mass, and liters to measure volume. In this system, each unit of measurement increases or decreases in multiples of ten. There are special prefixes like "kilo" and "deci" that show the value of each measurement unit.

KILO	HECTO	DECA	BASE UNIT	DECI	CENTI	MILLI
10 × 10 × 10 × LARGER than the base unit	10 × 10 × LARGER than the base unit	10 × LARGER than the base unit	METER LITER GRAM	10 × SMALLER than the base unit	10 × 10 × SMALLER than the base unit	10 × 10 × 10 × SMALLER than the base unit
1 kilo = 1,000 base units	1 hecto = 100 base units	1 deca = 10 base units	1 unit	10 deci = 1 unit	100 centi = 1 unit	1,000 milli = 1 unit

To convert larger units to smaller units, use multiplication. For example, to convert meters to centimeters, multiply the number of base units you have by 100 (10 × 10):

4 METERS = 4 × 100 (OR 10 × 10) = 400 CENTIMETERS

To convert smaller units to larger units, use division. For example, to convert meters to kilometers, divide the number of base units by 1,000 (10 × 10 × 10):

4,000 METERS = 4,000 ÷ 1,000 (OR 10 × 10 × 10) = 4 KILOMETERS

MULTIPLY—DECIMAL TO THE RIGHT →

← **DIVIDE—DECIMAL TO THE LEFT**

Use a shortcut! Convert units by moving the decimal to the right (to reach smaller units) or to the left (to reach larger units). To divide, move the decimal to the left. To multiply, move the decimal to the right.

Divide/multiply by 10	Divide/multiply by 100	Divide/multiply by 1,000
Move the decimal 1 time	Move the decimal 2 times	Move the decimal 3 times

ACTIVITY

These builders are struggling with different units of measurement. Choose the correct size of each item they need in order to finish the house.

Circle the correct door, window, and roof beam that will fit.

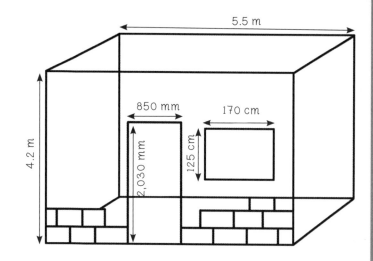

5.5 m

4.2 m

850 mm

2,030 mm

170 cm

125 cm

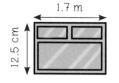
1.7 m
12.5 cm

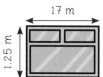
17 m
1.25 m

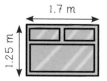
1.7 m
1.25 m

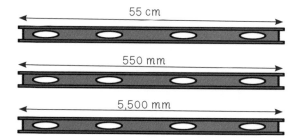
55 cm
550 mm
5,500 mm

How many rows of bricks will the builder need to lay from the bottom to the top of the house?

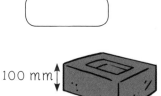

100 mm

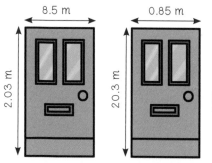
8.5 m
2.03 m

0.85 m
20.3 m

85 cm
203 cm

ACTIVITY

These three bags of sand need to be unloaded by order of weight.

Fill in the missing weight conversions on the bags. Then write down the order in which the bags should be unloaded, from heaviest to lightest.

A
1,000 g
=
.... kg

B
.... g
=
10 kg

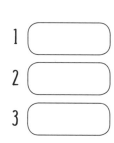
C
.... g
=
0.1 kg

1 [ ]

2 [ ]

3 [ ]

SPORTS DAY

Can you imagine a sports competition without numbers? It would be chaos! Without math, there would be no way of measuring how far someone had run, jumped, or thrown something. We wouldn't be able to compare speeds or heights or distances. We'd never know if someone had beaten his or her personal best or set a new world record.

ACTIVITY

These athletes are busy running, jumping, and throwing. Use your math skills to help them take part in the competition and to calculate the results!

HURDLES

There's only one hurdle on the track! Add the other hurdles by drawing one every seven meters in all three lanes.

JAVELIN

Five athletes are competing in the javelin throw. Read the following report, and then draw their javelins landing at the correct distances. Use colors to match each athlete's vest.

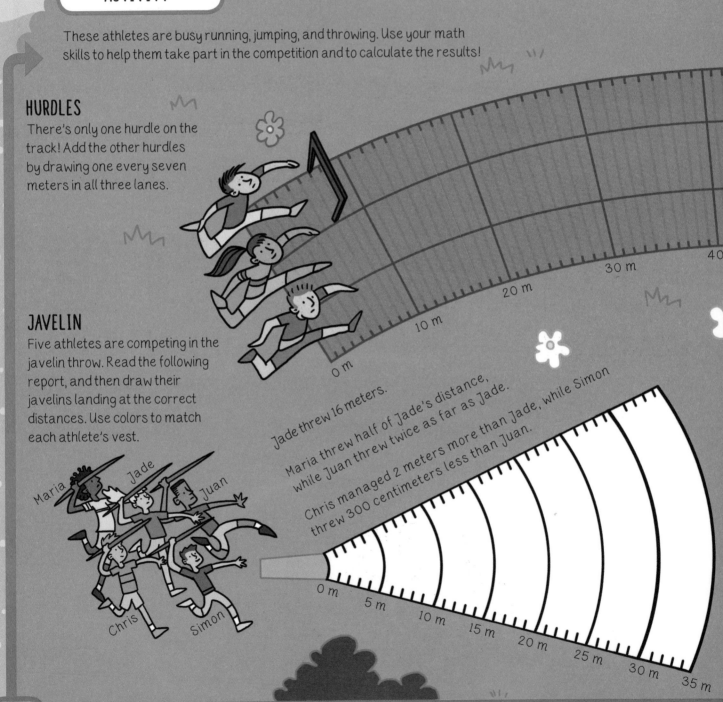

Jade threw 16 meters.

Maria threw half of Jade's distance, while Juan threw twice as far as Jade.

Chris managed 2 meters more than Jade, while Simon threw 300 centimeters less than Juan.

Maria Jade Juan

Chris Simon

CHECK THE ANSWERS AT THE BACK OF THE BOOK!

Ordinal numbers are 1st, 2nd, 3rd, etc. Ordinals indicate a position in relation to something else. These ordinals let the runners know what order, or position, they finished in the race.

SPRINT

Rank these runners according to their race results to show who came 1st, 2nd, 3rd, 4th, 5th, and 6th.

SPRINT: RESULTS		
Name	Time (seconds)	Position
Lucy	14.32	
Amir	14.23	
Alexander	14.01	
Rosa	14.10	
Tariq	14.31	
Imani	14.13	

HALF MARATHON

In the half marathon, the first three runners to cross the line receive medals. Convert their finishing times to hours, minutes, and seconds. Then color their medals gold, silver, or bronze!

HALF MARATHON RESULTS		
Name	Time	Time in hours, minutes, seconds
Salma	79 minutes 22 seconds	...... h ...... m ...... s
Zara	125 minutes 51 seconds	...... h ...... m ...... s
Ben	120 minutes 30 seconds	...... h ...... m ...... s

BEN
SALMA
ZARA

WILDLIFE WATCH

Keeping track of data is one of the most important jobs a scientist has. Data has to be accurate so that people can trust the outcome of experiments. To help us keep track of data, and to compare and analyze it, we use math skills to present it in charts, tables, or pictograms.

Check out this one-month survey of wildlife on a nature reserve in the Amazon rain forest. Now that you have all your data, you need to figure out what it means! This table shows how many sloths, snakes, and butterflies were spotted in the four different areas of the reserve.

	Sloths	Snakes	Butterflies
North	2	15	65
South	0	11	97
East	4	23	124
West	0	18	56

How many snakes did you spot in the eastern area?

How many creatures in total did you spot in the northern area?

How many sloths did you see in the whole reserve?

Which animal is the most common?

ACTIVITY

This chart shows what a group of monkeys ate in one day. One picture in the chart equals four food items in real life.

 = 4 passion fruits

 = 4 nuts

 = 4 leaves

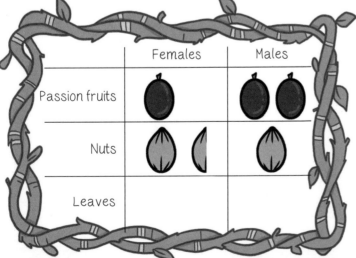

	Females	Males
Passion fruits		
Nuts		
Leaves		

How many passion fruits did the male monkeys eat?

How many nuts did the females eat?

How many passion fruits were eaten all together?

How many passion fruits and nuts did the females eat all together?

Fill in the correct amount of leaf symbols to show that the females ate 12 leaves and the males ate 10.

CHECK THE ANSWERS AT THE BACK OF THE BOOK!

ACTIVITY

A researcher charted birds for one week. Every time she saw a bird, she drew a straight line. For the fifth bird, she drew a diagonal line through the other four lines. This groups five together so she can count her total numbers by five.

On Thursday, the data was left off. She saw 6 green parrots and 12 blue ones. Mark the tally in the chart.

How many green parrots were charted on Wednesday? [ ]

On which day did the researcher record the most blue parrots? [ ]

How many parrots in total were observed on the weekend? [ ]

How many green parrots were recorded all together? [ ]

	Green parrots	Blue parrots
Monday	ⅢⅠ	ⅢⅠ ‖
Tuesday	ⅢⅠ ⅢⅠ ⅢⅠ ‖‖	ⅢⅠ ⅢⅠ ‖
Wednesday	ⅢⅠ ⅢⅠ Ⅰ	‖
Thursday		
Friday	ⅢⅠ ⅢⅠ ⅢⅠ ⅢⅠ Ⅰ	ⅢⅠ ⅢⅠ ⅢⅠ ‖
Saturday	‖‖	ⅢⅠ Ⅰ
Sunday	ⅢⅠ ‖	‖

ACTIVITY

A pie chart shows how one large group is divided up. The whole pie represents the whole group, or 100%. One half represents 50% and a quarter is 25%.

This pie chart shows how the reserve's population of river animals is divided into different species. Choose a color for each animal type, and color in the key. Then color the pie chart to show the correct proportions.

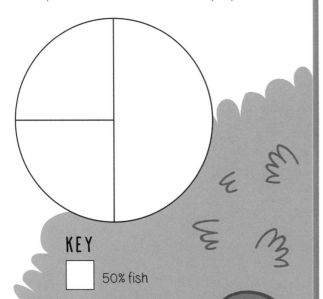

KEY

[ ] 50% fish

[ ] 25% reptiles

[ ] 25% amphibians

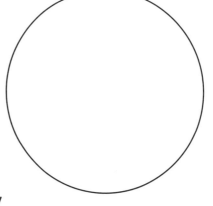

Complete this pie chart and key to show how the reserve's parrot population is divided up. Half of them are green parrots, one quarter are blue, and one quarter are red.

KEY

[ ] 50% [ ]

[ ] 25% [ ]

[ ] 25% [ ]

FIRST-RATE RATIOS

Ratios help us compare amounts. If the ratio of emperor penguins to Adélie penguins on an iceberg is 1:2, it means that for every one emperor penguin, there are two Adélie penguins. So if the iceberg is home to 10 emperor penguins, there would be 20 Adélie penguins. The ratio 10:20 is the same as 1:2, but ten times bigger.

RATIO RULES

To keep the same ratio, multiply both sides of the ratio by the same number.

x10   x10

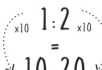
$$x10 \quad \frac{1:2}{=} \quad x10$$
$$10:20$$

 :

ACTIVITY

Draw the correct number of animals for each ratio.

1   RATIO OF TIGERS TO LIONS
2:3

 :

2   RATIO OF ANTS TO BEETLES
4:2

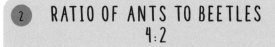

 :

3   RATIO OF SEALS TO SHARKS
3:1

  :

 :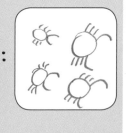

42

ACTIVITY

Recipes use ratios to combine great tastes in just the right amounts.
Write down a ratio for each pair of ingredients.
The first ingredient is provided on the shelf. Choose the correct amount
of the second ingredient to get the recipe just right, and circle it.

INGREDIENTS FOR THAI RED CURRY

4 parts coconut milk to
1 part water

coconut milk : water

4 parts chili powder to
2 parts coriander powder

chili powder : coriander powder

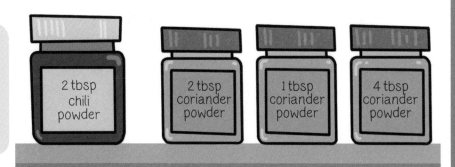

2 parts green beans to
3 parts red peppers

green beans : red peppers

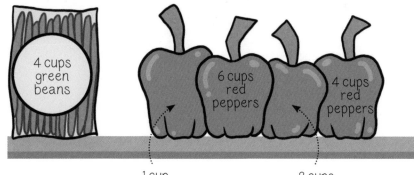

1 cup
red peppers   2 cups
red peppers

3 times as many cloves of
garlic as whole onions

cloves of garlic : whole onions

1 whole onion   2 cloves of garlic   4 cloves of garlic   3 cloves of garlic

TREASURE HUNT

Maps are a type of graph with vertical and horizontal lines. These lines are numbered by a horizontal *x*-axis and a vertical *y*-axis. Coordinates pinpoint where the lines cross each other. Coordinates are very useful for finding out where things are!

ACTIVITY

VOLCANO ISLAND

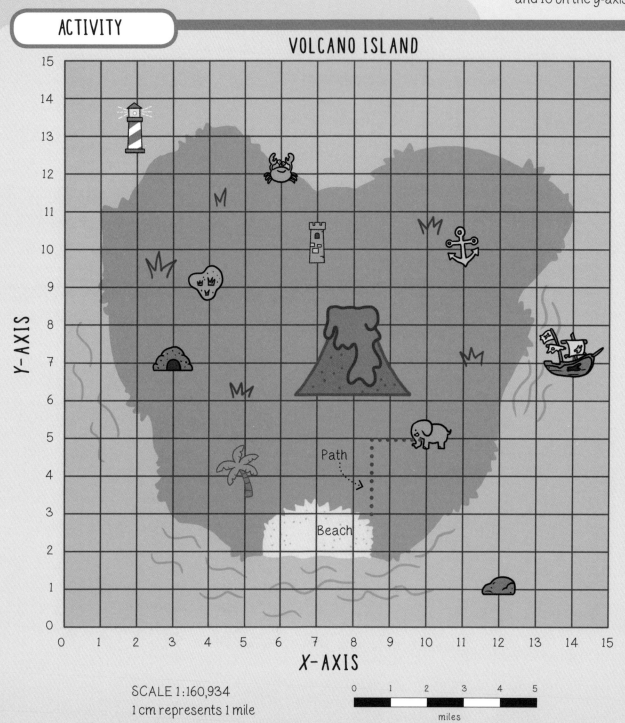

Path

Beach

Y-AXIS

X-AXIS

SCALE 1:160,934
1 cm represents 1 mile

0 1 2 3 4 5
miles

1 Look at the Volcano Island map. Find these coordinate points on the map and write down what feature can be found there. Remember, the first number is the x-coordinate, and the second is the y-coordinate.

(8, 8)

(10, 5)

(11, 10)

(6, 12)

2 Take the first letter of each answer above. Unscramble the letters to figure out a clue about where hidden treasure can be found.

Now write down the coordinates for the buried treasure:

3 Now write down the coordinates for these things:

Palm tree

Sea rock

Swamp

Lighthouse

KATHERINE JOHNSON

As you figure out coordinates by counting along the map, think about when humans had to perform long, complicated math calculations before computers. American mathematician Katherine Johnson (born in 1918), who worked for NASA, calculated the flight paths of spacecraft by hand. She loved to count: "Anything that could be counted, I did."

4 A scale bar gives a ratio that shows the relationship between the unit on the map and the actual measurement of the area in the real world.

Find the scale bar on the map. It shows that one square on the map represents 1 mile in real life. Use it to figure out the answers to these questions. Write your answers in miles.

How long is the beach?

How wide is the island from west to east at its widest point?

How long is the path between the beach and the elephant statue?

How far is it from the tower to the anchor?

45

PERFECT POLYGONS

A polygon is a flat shape with at least three straight sides. A vertex is where two sides meet on a polygon. Flat shapes are 2-D, which means that they have two dimensions—length and width.

ACTIVITY

Fill in the key below. Then use it to color the polygons in the picture to find out what animal is hiding in the jungle.

KEY	How many sides?	How many vertices?
▲ Triangle		
■ Square		
▬ Rectangle		

	How many sides?	How many vertices?
⬠ Pentagon		
⬡ Hexagon		

A quadrilateral is a polygon with 4 sides. Which 2 polygons on this page are quadrilaterals?

UNDERSTANDING AREA

Area is the amount of space inside a polygon. Imagine the area of a rectangle or square as the number of equal-sized or identical squares that would fit inside it.

To calculate the area, multiply the width by the length. For example, this rectangle is 2 squares wide by 4 squares long. Its area is $2 \times 4 = 8$ squares. Count them up to check!

Length = 4

Width = 2

ACTIVITY

Welcome to Rectangle Farm! Fill in the two missing field lengths, and then complete the calculation in each field to solve the area.

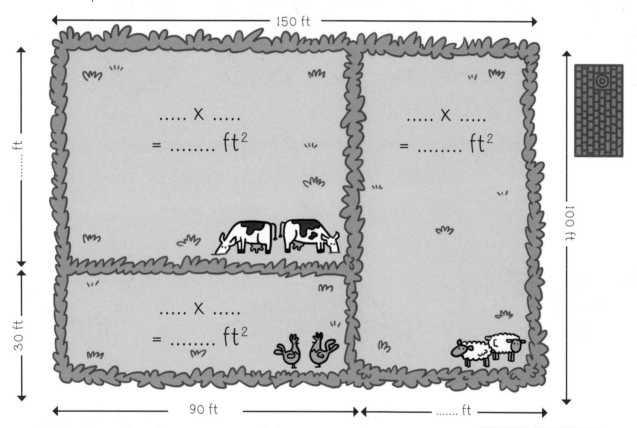

150 ft

..... × .....

= .... ft^2

..... × .....

= .... ft^2

..... × .....

= .... ft^2

100 ft

..... ft

30 ft

90 ft

.... ft

What is the total area of the farm? Add the area of each field to find out.

Perimeter is the distance around the edge of a shape. It's the total length of all the sides. The farmer needs new fencing for the perimeter of the whole farm. How much does she need? Add the lengths of each side to find out.

MATH TIP

The unit for area is always written as a square because it shows how many squares fit in the object. Write square feet as ft^2, and square inches as in^2.

SUPER SYMMETRY

A line of symmetry divides a shape into two identical halves.
Each half is the mirror image of the other.

ACTIVITY

Draw lines of symmetry onto each of these everyday objects.
We've done the first one for you.

triangle

square

pentagon

hexagon

heptagon

octagon

ACTIVITY

Which of these bird shapes is not symmetrical?

CHECK THE ANSWERS AT THE BACK OF THE BOOK!

ACTIVITY

Complete these images. Make some symmetrical and others not!

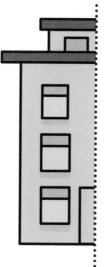

ARCHIMEDES

Geometry is the study of shapes. The great Greek mathematician Archimedes (c. 287–212 B.C.E.) made many breakthroughs in geometry, including how to measure the surface area of a sphere (ball). He would work for days—drawing diagrams and scribbling theories—without stopping to eat, drink, or bathe!

PIECES OF PI

A circle is a closed shape, but it is not a polygon because it has no straight sides. The unique nature of a circle is explained with a special number known as pi. (Sorry—you can't eat this pi!)

Whatever the size of a circle, if you divide its circumference by its diameter, the answer is always an infinite number called pi. Pi is 3.14159…. This number is named after the Greek letter "p" and its symbol is π.

— Radius

— Diameter (2 x radius)

— The distance around the edge of a circle is called the circumference.

MATH TIP

We use rounding to make it easier to do calculations using pi. Pi is usually rounded to the nearest hundredth: 3.14.

ACTIVITY

If you know the diameter of a circle, you can use pi to work out its circumference:

CIRCUMFERENCE = DIAMETER × π

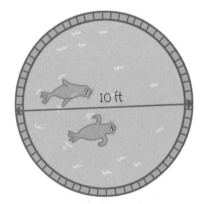

10 ft

At the zoo, the seals live in a pool that is surrounded by a circular fence. We know that the diameter of the circle is 10 feet. So, in the formula, we can substitute the numbers we know:

CIRCUMFERENCE = 10 × 3.14 = 31.4 FT

At the zoo, the fences around the penguin and crocodile pools need to be replaced. What's the circumference of each pool? Use a calculator to multiply if you need help.

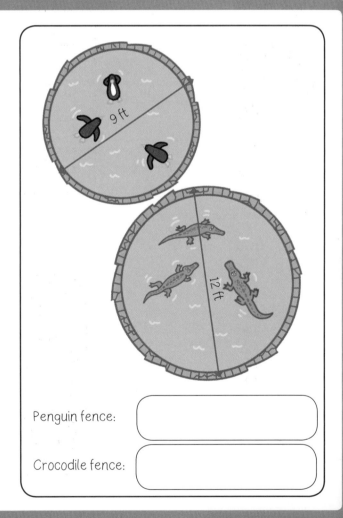

9 ft

12 ft

Penguin fence: [   ]

Crocodile fence: [   ]

CHECK THE ANSWERS AT THE BACK OF THE BOOK!

ACTIVITY

You are in charge of a mission to send rockets to circumnavigate three planets, so you can learn more about each of them. To do this, you'll need to use circumference to calculate the rockets' paths around the planets Zog, Zag, and Zig.

> The radius of a circle is the distance in a straight line from the center to the outside edge. So, the radius is half the diameter, or:
>
> ## DIAMETER = RADIUS × 2

ZOG — 900 miles

ZAG — 2,000 miles

ZIG — 2,500 miles

ROCKET A
Fuel capacity to travel 3,000 miles.

ROCKET B
Fuel capacity to travel 8,000 miles.

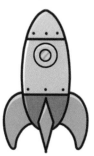

ROCKET C
Fuel capacity to travel 7,000 miles.

Calculate and record the circumference trajectory that each rocket would have to travel in order to fly around each planet on its research mission. Then pick the rocket with the right amount of fuel to complete the mission.

	ZOG	ZAG	ZIG
Circumference (Diameter x π)			
Assigned rocket			

AWESOME ANGLES

An angle is the space between two crossing lines. We measure angles in units called degrees (°). There are 360° in a circle.

A protractor measures angles.

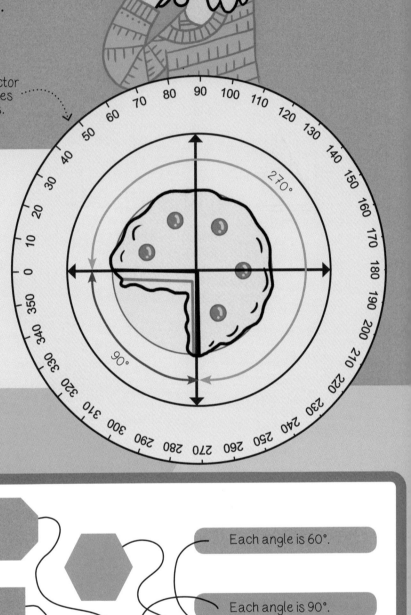

Protractors are very useful objects. You can use them to measure angles in shapes like triangles and squares—even cakes!

In this cake, a large piece is missing. You can see from the numbers marked on the protractor that the angle of the missing piece is 90°.

The angle of the remaining cake is 270°.

ACTIVITY

The angles inside regular polygons are different depending on the shape. Follow the lines to find out how big they are!

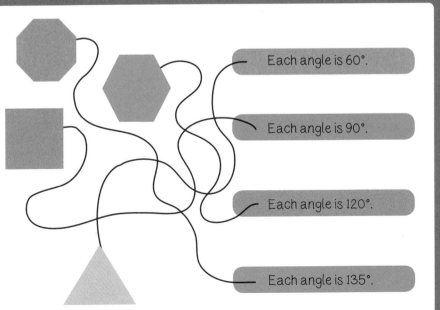

Each angle is 60°.

Each angle is 90°.

Each angle is 120°.

Each angle is 135°.

DID YOU KNOW?

Regular polygons are shapes with sides that are all the same length.

CHECK THE ANSWERS AT THE BACK OF THE BOOK!

ACTIVITY

Programming codes often use angle measurements for instructions. The code on the right uses 90° rotations to turn the car to the right.

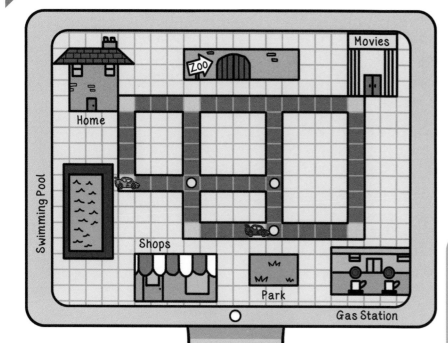

KEY & CODES

○ traffic circle

▢ parking space

F1 = forward 1 space (the number tells you how many spaces the car should move)

90 = 90° turn

180 = 180° turn

270 = 270° turn

360 = 360° turn

MATH TIP

Angles are measured in a clockwise direction, so:

- a 90° turn is 1 rotation to the right,
- a 180° turn is 2 rotations to the right, and
- a 270° turn is 3 rotations to the right.

Use the key to follow these programming commands. Start at the swimming pool each time. Where does the blue car end up? Record your answer.

1. F4, 90, F3

2. F4, 270, F5

3. F9, 270, F5, 90, F5

4. Now write some code to program the red car to move from the park to home, with a stop for gas on the way.

ADA LOVELACE

Lovelace was a female mathematician. In 1843, she wrote the first program for a computer, which was referred to as an "Analytical Engine."

53

TRICKY TRIANGLES

A triangle is a 2-D (two-dimensional) shape with three sides. The three angles inside a triangle always add up to 180°. There are four main types of triangles.

EQUILATERAL

An equilateral triangle has three sides that are the same length. Each inside angle is the same size.

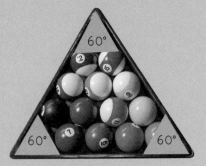

RIGHT TRIANGLE

A right triangle has one angle that is 90°.

90°

ISOSCELES

An isosceles triangle has two sides that are equal in length.

Two of the inside angles are the same size.

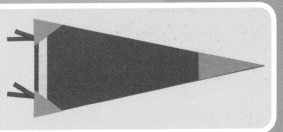

SCALENE

A scalene triangle has three sides that are different lengths. All three inside angles are different sizes.

ACTIVITY

Draw some triangular sails to suit each boat!

Isosceles

Scalene

Equilateral

Right triangle

CHECK THE ANSWERS AT THE BACK OF THE BOOK!

ACUTE AND OBTUSE

An angle that is less than 90° is called acute.

An angle more than 90° but less than 180° is obtuse.

Acute angle

Obtuse angle

ACTIVITY

How many triangles can you spot in the city?

3-D SHAPES

This cereal box is not a flat 2-D shape. It has three dimensions—length (or height), width, and depth—so it is 3-D. It's called a cuboid, which is a 3-D shape that has 6 rectangular faces. When those faces are square, like a die, it is called a cube.

Length
30 cm

Depth
10 cm

Width
20 cm

A 3-D shape has volume—the amount of space inside it. Volume can be measured in units of centimeters cubed (cm³) or meters cubed (m³).

To calculate the volume of a cube or cuboid, use this equation:

VOLUME = LENGTH × WIDTH × DEPTH

ACTIVITY

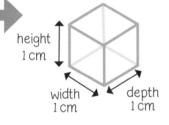

height
1 cm

width
1 cm

depth
1 cm

This die is 1 cm long,
1 cm wide, and 1 cm deep.

Its volume is $1 \times 1 \times 1 = 1\,cm^3$.

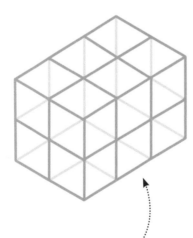

How many dice will fit inside this cuboid?
You can check your answer using the volume equation.

Can you calculate the volume of the cereal box at the top of the page? Don't forget the unit of measurement!

If you opened the cereal box, you would get the 2-D shape shown below. This is called a net. A net is like a flattened box that you can fold up to make a 3-D shape.

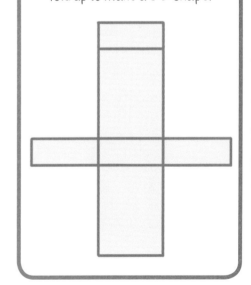

1 Abdi has different shaped boxes to pack up his homemade chocolates one by one. The boxes come to him flat and he has to build them. Help him identify the 3-D shape that each of these flat boxes will make when he's finished building them. Circle the correct shape for each one.

A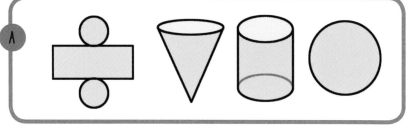

B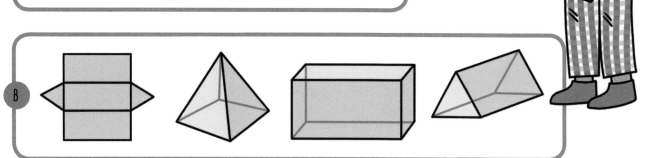

C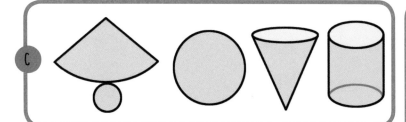

D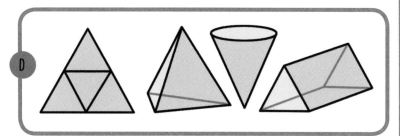

E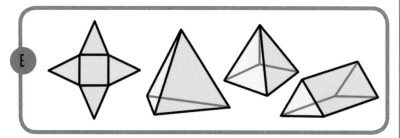

2 Abdi has to order cube-shaped boxes for a special delivery. Which of these nets will NOT make a cube?

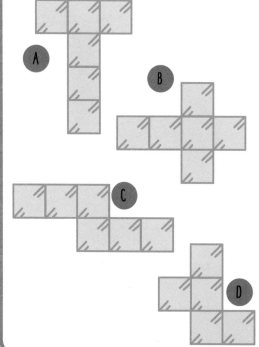

A

B

C

D

57

TRANSFORMATION

Objects can keep many of their original properties but can be transformed for new effects. Graphic designers use computer software to transform images all the time. Here are some examples of how shapes can be transformed.

Mirror line

Reflection flips an image over an imaginary "mirror line." The reflected image faces the opposite direction of the original image.

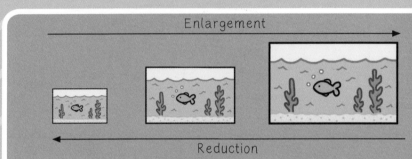

Enlargement

Reduction

Enlargement increases the size of a shape but keeps its proportions. Reduction shrinks the size of an object but keeps its proportions. If you don't maintain the proportions, the object will be distorted.

Rotation turns an object around a point of rotation.

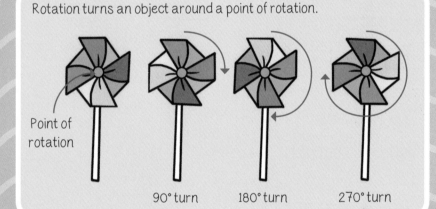

Point of rotation

90° turn   180° turn   270° turn

Translation is when an object stays the same shape, size, and angle but moves, or "slides," in any direction.

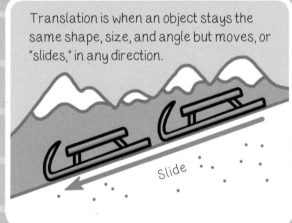

Slide

ACTIVITY

Draw this mug's reflection. Make sure it is the same distance from the mirror line as the original.

Rotate this flag and pole by 180°.

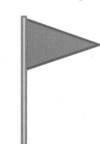

CHECK THE ANSWERS AT THE BACK OF THE BOOK!

ACTIVITY

Imagine you're a graphic designer. You have altered a photograph to make a new scene for a travel magazine. The magazine editor wants to know all about the transformations so she can get permission from the photographer to use the transformed image. Explain the images below.

BEFORE

AFTER

Original photograph

Transformed photograph

Translation:

Reduction:

Rotation:

Enlargement:

Reflection:

Slide this dog diagonally upward to the right.

Enlarge this kite.

GET TESSELLATING!

A tessellation is a repeating pattern of shapes, but not just any shapes! In a tessellation, there cannot be any gaps between the shapes. This means that if we want to tessellate using just one regular polygon, it has to be a triangle, square, or hexagon.

ACTIVITY

Finish coloring the square tessellation of this chessboard.

Continue the color pattern of this tiled floor's triangular tessellation. Does the floor look 3-D?

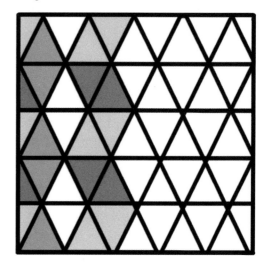

Add some more wax cells to this tessellating hexagonal honeycomb.

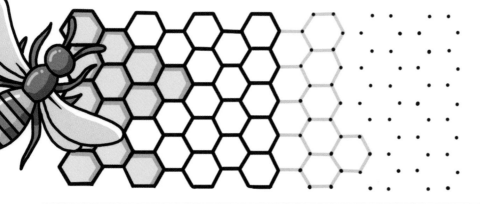

Bees build honeycombs of hexagons because these shapes can be packed tightly, creating the most cells with the least amount of wax.

Tessellations can use more than one regular polygon.

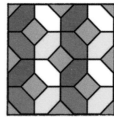

CHECK THE ANSWERS AT THE BACK OF THE BOOK!

THE BIG MATH QUIZ

Now it's time to test your skills to see if you really are a math master!

1 What is the number 3,721 written out in expanded form?

a) 3,000 + 700 + 20 + 2 ☐

b) 3,000 + 700 + 30 + 1 ☐

c) 3,000 + 700 + 20 + 1 ☐

2 What's the name given to numbers that are below zero?

a) Negative ☐

b) Subzero ☐

c) Negatory ☐

3 On a smartphone, computer, or calculator, how is the multiplication symbol often shown?

a) * ☐

b) # ☐

c) $ ☐

4 What does GCF stand for?

a) Greatest creeping factor ☐

b) Greatest common factor ☐

c) Greatest common factory ☐

5 What is the name of the insect that lays its eggs at prime-number intervals?

a) Cricket ☐

b) Caterpillar ☐

c) Cicada ☐

CHECK THE ANSWERS AT THE BACK OF THE BOOK!

6 What is the name of the number that is above the line in a fraction?

a) Denominator

b) Calculator

c) Numerator

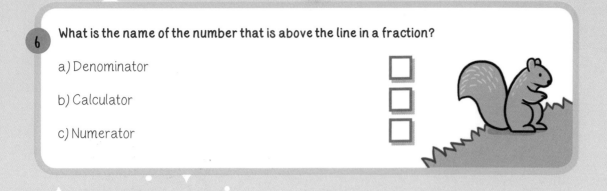

7 How do you write 2,010 in Roman numerals?

a) MPQ

b) MMX

c) MMV

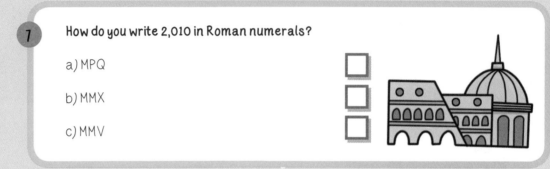

8 What is the name of the number that is used to find out the circumference of a circle?

a) Pi

b) Cake

c) Cookie

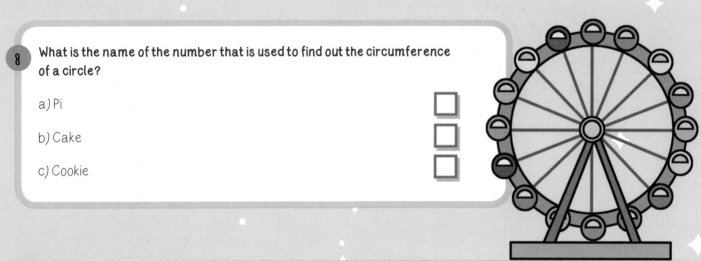

9 Which of these is not a type of triangle?

a) Equilateral

b) Isosceles

c) Extreme

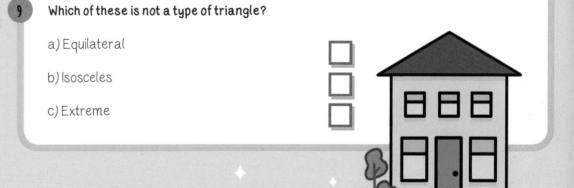

CHECK THE ANSWERS AT THE BACK OF THE BOOK!

ANSWERS

Page 8
COOL COLUMNS
3,725 becomes 3,000 + 700 + 20 + 5
4,159 becomes 4,000 + 100 + 50 + 9
7,022 becomes 7,000 + 0 + 20 + 2

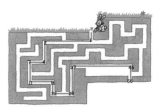

The pattern of increasing numbers is +1, +2, +3, +4, +5, +6, +7, +8, +9, +10.

Page 9
SUPER SUMS
Road Sign 1
School to train station = 5 miles (7 − 2)
Train station to hospital = 3 miles (10 − 7)
School to hospital = 8 miles (10 − 2)

Road Sign 2
Park to bus station = 5 miles (18 − 13)
Bus station to supermarket = 2 miles (20 − 18)
Park to supermarket = 7 miles (20 − 13)

Pages 10–11
POPULATION COUNT
Addington
1. 121 2. 430 3. 132 4. 9,443
5. 1,314 6. 15,416
Total population: 26,856

Subtractington
1. 18 2. 38 3. 509 4. 396 5. 5,482
6. 64,963
Total population: 71,406

44,550 more people live in Subtractington than Addington (71,406 − 26,856).

Pages 12–13
ABOVE AND BELOW ZERO

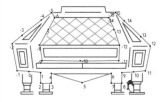

Sunrise: 32 + 8 = 40°F (0 + 8 = 8°C)
Midday: 40 − 11 = 29°F (8 − 11 = −3°C)
Afternoon: 29 + 5 = 34°F (−3 + 5 = 2°C)
Nightfall: 34 − 7 = 27°F (2 − 7 = −5°C)

Pages 14–15
MULTIPLY AND SUPPLY
Filling the Orders
2 packs of frisbees: 2 × $8 = $16
2 crates of basketballs: 2 × $9 = $18
2 tubes of tennis balls: 2 × $7 = $14

Increasing the Orders
Summer camp: $16 × 2 = $32
Sporting goods store: $18 × 3 = $54
School: $14 × 4 = $56

Pages 16–17
MEET THE MULTIPLES

Number	Price	Total
7 boxes of hamster food	$10	$70
5 boxes of cat food	$6	$30
6 boxes of dog bones	$4	$24
Grand total:		$124

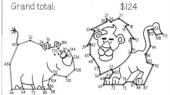

Pages 18–19
SHARE AND DIVIDE
Outdoor Adventure
Fisher's backpack: 1 water bottle; 2 energy bars; 11 grapes; 3 bananas; 4 worms; 2 hooks
Tent maker's backpack: 1 water bottle; 2 energy bars; 11 grapes; 3 bananas; 13 sticks; 3 coils of rope

Sharing Marshmallows
3 × 26 = 78 marshmallows in total
78 ÷ 5 = 15 marshmallows per child, with 3 remaining
78 ÷ 10 = 7 marshmallows per child, with 8 remaining

Pages 20–21
FACTOR FACTORY
Factors of 9: 1, 9, 3
Factors of 14: 1, 14, 2, 7
Factors of 21: 1, 21, 3, 7
The GCF of 14 and 21 is 7.

Book Packs
Mr. 12:
4 × 3-pack of books = $40
OR
3 × 4-pack of books = $36
3 × 4-pack of books is cheaper.

Mrs. 15:
5 × 3-pack of books (5 × $10 = $50)
OR
3 × 5-pack of books (3 × $14 = $42)
3 × 5-pack of books is cheaper.

Mr. 20:
5 × 4-pack of books (5 × $12 = $60)
OR
4 × 5-pack of books (4 × $14 = $56)
4 × 5-pack of books is cheaper.

Mrs. 21:
7 × 3-pack of books (7 × $10 = $70)
OR
3 × 7-pack of books (3 × $18 = $54)
3 × 7-pack of books is cheaper.

Pages 22–23
NUMBERS IN THEIR PRIME
Color in all the fish except 61, 103, 23, 7, 67, 43, and 13.

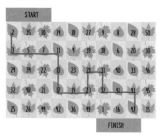

Pages 24–25
CRACK THE CODE
1. 23, 27, 31, 35, 39, **43**
   1, 2, 4, 8, 16, **32**
   20, 15, 11, 8, 6, **5**
   12, 24, 36, 48, 60, **72**
2. The riddle describes the middle padlock. The numbers add up to 7 (2 + 4 + 1).
3. The sum total is 14. The line cuts through 10 and 4.
4. 21 (add the two previous numbers 13 + 8).
5. Shortest route = Earth to C to A to B to Earth OR Earth to B to A to C to Earth. Time taken 14 seconds (2 + 4 + 5 + 3 OR 3 + 5 + 4 + 2)

Encryption
Challenge 1 in letters: W, I, L, Y
Challenges 2, 3, 4, and 5 in letters: R, O, C, O
The thief's name is Wily Roco.

Pages 26–27
FOOD FRACTIONS
Sharing Pizza

CHUN $\frac{3}{12}$

RUBY $\frac{6}{12}$

SANJAY $\frac{2}{12}$

There is 1 slice left.

Squirrels

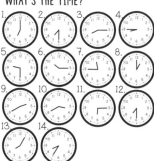

Pages 28–29
DECIMALS THAT DIVIDE
Crossing the Gorge
$2\frac{1}{2}$ → 2.5
$9\frac{1}{4}$ → 9.25
3.25 → $3\frac{1}{4}$
0.75 → $\frac{3}{4}$
$1\frac{3}{4}$ → 1.75

Shopping List
Total = $7.65
$10.00 − $7.65 = $2.35 change

Pages 30–31
PERCENTAGES
LOADING...25%
LOADING...90%
LOADING...75%

Food Percentages
Water = 50%, $\frac{5}{10} = \frac{1}{2}$, 0.5
Eggs = 25%, $\frac{25}{100} = \frac{1}{4}$, 0.25
Cake = 75%, $\frac{75}{100} = \frac{3}{4}$, 0.75

Pages 32–33
WHAT'S THE TIME?

Pages 34–35
ROMAN NUMERALS

Roman Years
1. MMX = 2010
2. MMXXIX = 2029
3. MMLXIV = 2064

Number Search
1. DCCLIII
2. LXIV
3. LXXX
4. CCCXCV

Page 37
MEASURING METRIC
Building Parts
Correct door: 85 cm by 203 cm
Correct window: 1.25 m by 1.7 m
Correct beam: 5,500 mm
Bricks: 42 (4.2 m = 420 cm = 4,200 mm; 4,200 ÷ 100 = 42)

Bags of Sand
Bag A 1,000 g = 1 kg
Bag B 10,000 g = 10 kg
Bag C 100 g = 0.1 kg
Unloading order: B, A, C.

Pages 38–39
SPORTS DAY
Hurdles

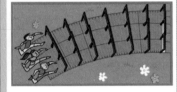

Javelin
Jade: 16 meters; Maria: 8 meters;
Juan: 32 meters; Chris: 18 meters;
Simon: 29 meters

Sprint

Name	Time (seconds)	Position
Lucy	14.32	6th
Amir	14.23	4th
Alexander	14.01	1st
Rosa	14.10	2nd
Tariq	14.31	5th
Imani	14.13	3rd

Half Marathon

Name	Time	Time in hours, minutes, seconds
Salma	79 minutes 22 seconds	1 h 19 m 22 s
Zara	125 minutes 51 seconds	2 h 5 m 51 s
Ben	120 minutes 30 seconds	2 h 0 m 30 s

Gold = Salma
Silver = Ben
Bronze = Zara

Pages 40–41
WILDLIFE WATCH
Sloths, Snakes, and Butterflies
Snakes in the eastern area: 23
Total creatures in the northern area: 82
Sloths in the whole reserve: 6
Most common animal: butterfly

Monkeys
Passion fruits eaten by males: 8
Nuts eaten by females: 6
Passion fruits eaten in total: 12
Passion fruits and nuts eaten by females: 10
Leaf symbols: draw 3 for the female monkeys and 2½ for the male monkeys

Birds
Green parrots = ℋℋ I
Blue parrots = ℋℋ ℋℋ II
Green parrots on Wednesday: 11
Most blue parrots: Friday
Parrots in total on the weekend: 18
Green parrots all together = 71

River Animals   Parrot Colors

Pages 42–43
FIRST-RATE RATIOS
Animal Ratios
1. Draw 6 lions   2. Draw 4 beetles
3. Draw 3 sharks

Ingredient Ratios
Coconut milk : water = 4:2
Chili powder : coriander powder = 3:4
Green beans : red peppers = 2:3
Cloves of garlic : whole onions = 3:1

Pages 44–45
TREASURE HUNT
1. (8, 8) = volcano
(10, 5) = elephant statue
(11, 10) = anchor
(6, 12) = crab
2. The treasure is in the cave (3, 7).
3. Palm tree = (5, 4)
Sea rock = (12, 1)
Swamp = (4, 9)
Lighthouse = (2, 13)
4. Beach = 3 miles long
Island width = 14 miles
Path = 3.5 miles
Tower to anchor = 4 miles

Pages 46–47
PERFECT POLYGONS
Hidden Animal

	Sides	Vertices
Triangle	3	3
Square	4	4
Rectangle	4	4
Pentagon	5	5
Hexagon	6	6

The square and rectangle are both quadrilaterals.

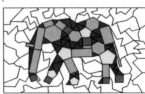

Understanding Area
Missing field lengths: cow field 70 ft; sheep field 60 ft.
Cow field area: 70 × 90 = 6,300 ft²
Chicken field area: 30 × 90 = 2,700 ft²
Sheep field area: 60 × 100 = 6,000 ft²
Total area of the farm: 6,300 + 2,700 + 6,000 = 15,000 ft² OR 150 × 100 = 15,000 ft²
Perimeter: 150 + 100 + 150 + 100 = 500 ft OR 100 + 150 + 70 + 30 + 90 + 60 = 500 ft

Page 48
SUPER SYMMETRY
Lines of Symmetry

Symmetrical Birds

Pages 50–51
PIECES OF PI
Zoo
Circumference of penguin pool:
9 × 3.14 = 28.26 ft
Circumference of crocodile pool:
12 × 3.14 = 37.68 ft

Planets
ZOG circumference: 2,826 miles
Assigned rocket: A
ZAG circumference: 6,280 miles
Assigned rocket: C
ZIG circumference: 7,850 miles
Assigned rocket: B

Pages 52–53
AWESOME ANGLES
Regular Polygons
Triangle: each angle is 60°
Square: each angle is 90°
Hexagon: each angle is 120°
Octagon: each angle is 135°

Car Coding
1. Store
2. Zoo
3. Movies
4. F5, 270, F8, 270, F14

Pages 54–55
TRICKY TRIANGLES
Sailing Boats

Isosceles   Scalene   Equilateral   Right triangle

Triangles in the City: 26 in total

Pages 56–57
3-D SHAPES
Volume
12 dice would fit in the cuboid. Volume is 12 cm³ (3 × 2 × 2).
The volume of the cereal box is 6,000 cm³ (30 × 20 × 10).

Chocolate Boxes
1. A. Cylinder
B. Triangular prism
C. Cone
D. Triangular pyramid
E. Square-bottom pyramid
2. Net D would not make a cube.

Pages 58–59
TRANSFORMATION
Transforming Objects

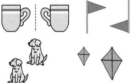

Altered Image
Translation: Tree has moved left
Reduction: Cloud has reduced in size
Rotation: Flying bird has been rotated
Enlargement: Sun has enlarged
Reflection: Boat has been reflected

Page 60
GET TESSELLATING!

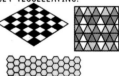

Pages 61–62
THE BIG MATH QUIZ
1. c   2. a   3. a   4. b   5. c
6. c   7. b   8. a   9. c